Welcc

NAOMI STARKEY

Rock—something to be watched for when aboard a boat, especially in unfamiliar waters. Rock—the hidden barrier beneath a thin covering of soil that can thwart the most determined of farmers. Rock—blocking our metaphorical path, causing our feet to stumble.

Nevertheless, rock also signifies stability, a firm footing in marshy ground, stepping-stones across a stream. Jesus told the story of the house built on rock, which outlasted the storm because of its solid foundations. And some rocks can be split open to reveal extraordinary interiors—precious jewels and dazzling minerals. Something apparently dull and utilitarian is transformed into an object of breathtaking beauty.

'Rock bottom' is how we describe the lowest point, the worst moment, the place from which there seems no escape. Strangely enough, though, that very phrase contains its own comfort. Knowing that we are at rock bottom can be a relief. There is no further to fall; we are not hurtling into a bottomless pit.

Of course, rock bottom is far from the best place to be, but it's where we can start thinking of the possibility of ascent, of returning (even if slowly and painfully) to the light. Again and again the Bible describes God as 'rock'—a place of shelter, a refuge from the assaults of our enemies, a mountainous strength. If we are truly at rock bottom, we have come to the end of our human resources and can turn to God, the ground of our being.

Naomi Starkey

This compilation copyright © BRF 2007
Authors retain copyright in their own work
Illustrations copyright © Jane Bottomley, Ray Burrows and Ian Mitchell 2007

Published by
The Bible Reading Fellowship
First Floor, Elsfield Hall
15–17 Elsfield Way, Oxford OX2 8FG
Websites: www.brf.org.uk and www.quietspaces.org.uk
ISBN-10: 1 84101 498 2
ISBN-13: 978 1 84101 498 2

First published 2007
10 9 8 7 6 5 4 3 2 1 0

Acknowledgments
Unless otherwise stated, scripture quotations are taken from the Holy Bible, New International Version,
copyright © 1973, 1978, 1984 by International Bible Society, are used by permission of Hodder &
Stoughton, a division of Hodder Headline Ltd. All rights reserved. 'NIV' is a registered trademark of
International Bible Society. UK trademark number 1448790.

'Turnstones' by Barrie Armstrong, from *The Changing Face* (Athena Press, 2006).

A catalogue record for this book is available from the British Library

Printed by Gutenberg Press, Tarxien, Malta

Quiet Spaces

CONTENTS

Jewels from the Rock

Heather Coupland enjoys writing about everyday spirituality and is training to be a spiritual director. She has also written for 'Woman Alive' magazine and is a contributor to BRF's 'Day by Day with God' Bible reading notes.

I wonder what picture comes into your mind when you consider the word 'rock'? Is it the craggy and irregular coastline of a familiar holiday destination, or maybe the ancient and mysterious monument of Stonehenge? Do you think about the frustration of digging in the rocky, unyielding soil of your garden, or perhaps about the beauty of a well-established rockery, where rocks have been transformed into something worth looking at rather than being removed?

When we consider the use of the word 'rock' in scripture, we might think of verses like 'The Lord is my rock, my fortress and my deliverer; my God is my rock, in whom I take refuge' or 'For who is God besides the Lord? And who is the Rock except our God?' (Psalm 18:2, 31, NIV). In the Old Testament, particularly in the Psalms, there are many references to God as our rock. This imagery reassures us that our God can be a solid foundation for us to stand on when life seems precarious. He also provides us with a hiding place to run into and a shelter from the storm, which can't be demolished, however fierce the wind.

I was taking part in a discussion group recently where we were talking about different images of God and which ideas in the Bible we found helpful or unhelpful. We were given a list of verses to consider, each representing a different aspect of the character of God. One of them was the verse from Psalm 18 above: 'The Lord is my rock, my fortress… my shield and… my stronghold.' I have always found this a comforting picture, so I was surprised when some members of the group remarked that they didn't find the image of rock or fortress, in association with God, very helpful at all. For them, this picture was too hard and harsh, too far removed from everyday life to be of any benefit.

As I've considered the overall theme of God as our rock in the whole of scripture, I have been surprised by how versatile the image can be. It is interesting to note that sometimes the God who is portrayed as the rock on which we stand is made very personal by the use of phrases such as 'my rock' (see 2 Samuel 22:2–3) or 'our rock' (Deuteronomy 32:31). At other times, this rock stands apart simply as 'the Rock', representing God as solid and indestructible. In Deuteronomy 32 we even find that people can desert or reject the rock that is God, or can choose to be nourished by him as he provides for their needs.

I've been particularly struck by verses that speak of God bringing forth sustenance from the rock to help his people on their journey of faith. While the Israelites were wandering in the desert, Moses followed God's instructions and produced water for them to drink by striking a

God can be a solid foundation for us to stand on when life seems precarious

Beautiful crystals and semi-precious stones
can often be found behind the most
unattractive exteriors

We can receive God's promises to us, jewels hewn from the rock of his word, into our hearts

A hiding place to run into and a shelter from the storm

rock with his staff (Exodus 17:6). Numbers 20 even states that if Moses had had enough trust in God, he could have simply spoken to the rock and the water they needed would have been provided.

Before Moses died, he spoke of Israel's history and of how God had looked after the people through many trials and tribulations, how they had been fed with 'the fruit of the fields' and nourished with 'honey from the rock, and with oil from the flinty crag' (Deuteronomy 32:13). Psalm 81:16 echoes this theme, when God promises that if his people will listen and submit to him they will be 'fed with the finest of wheat' and with 'honey from the rock'.

From these varied references we can see that the image of rock in scripture doesn't have to be a picture of something cold and impersonal. We can come to our God the rock when we are weary and hungry, to find in him a place of refreshment and nourishment. We can come to this safe place and shout our praises (Psalm 95:1), surrounded by the shelter of walls that are impervious to the devil's battering rams. Jacob even found comfort in a good night's sleep with a rock for a pillow (Genesis 28:11). God surely must have performed a miracle for a rock to be that versatile!

As we move into the New Testament, the theme of rock is barely mentioned. Apart from Matthew 16:18, where Jesus speaks of Peter as the rock on which the Church is to be built, the most well-known reference is in Matthew 7:24–27, in the parable of the wise and foolish builders. In this story, the rock signifies Jesus' words. He wants to show people that anyone who puts his words into practice in their lives is building on a firm foundation that will not crumble, whatever they may have to endure.

As we learn to live each day standing firm on the rock that is our God and trusting in his words, what is the sustenance we can receive to keep us going on our walk with him? Just as the Israelites received water in the desert, surely we can receive God's promises to us, jewels hewn from the rock of his word, into our hearts.

My husband loves fossils and has a small collection of them in his study. I've learned through looking at them that the most beautiful crystals and semi-precious stones can often be found behind the most unattractive exteriors. He has several geodes, chunks of rock that look unappealing on the outside but which, when broken open, reveal a mass of sparkling, beautiful crystals. As we read our Bibles and perhaps follow Bible reading notes, we are giving God the opportunity to show us new jewels in the rock of his word. Sometimes we will experience a jewel sparkling out at us very obviously as we read; at other times we will have to work a little harder to find treasure in unexpected places. We can take these gems with us on our journey and let our hearts feed on them when times are hard.

For many of us, there will be particular 'jewels'—special verses that God has given us at a certain point in our lives. I'm certain that we could fill a whole issue of *Quiet Spaces* with verses that people have found especially pertinent or comforting at various points on their journey of faith. As I've talked to friends about writing this article, I've been delighted at how many of them can very readily quote a verse that holds real significance for them. For some it is a verse from their childhood that has been kept close to their hearts for many years. For others it might be a verse that God has brought alive to them as they've read their Bibles recently. It might be a verse that they had never really noticed before but which has had a significant impact on their lives because of its relevance to their immediate circumstances.

As I reflect on my own life, I realize that many verses have been very precious to me at different times over

The image of rock in scripture doesn't have to be a picture of something cold and impersonal the years. Many of these jewels from scripture came to me when I was low or discouraged or facing some kind of difficulty. God spoke to me in these situations through his word and did indeed give me a firm place to stand when my own foundations felt very shaky.

I think of the time after my daughter was born, when I suffered from post-natal depression. Psalm 139:7–12 came alive for me then in an incredible way. Even though I felt I was under a huge dark cloud, I clung on to verse 12 in particular, where the psalmist says, 'Even the darkness will not be dark to you; the night will shine like the day, for darkness is as light to you.' It was such a relief to know that even though I felt as if I was in darkness, God was not, and he was with me.

Many people I know have been blessed by the wonderful words in Jeremiah 29:11, where God says through the prophet, 'I know the plans I have for you… plans to prosper you and not to harm you, plans to give you hope and a future.' I often turn back to these words when I've lost my direction and feel as if my life is becoming unfocused. I take huge reassurance from the fact that God has a purpose for my life, even when I don't understand how he's going to work things out.

There are many well-known Bible verses that speak of comfort

Jacob even found comfort in a good night's sleep with a rock for a pillow

There are many well-known Bible verses that speak of comfort and reassurance in times of trouble and of God's presence with us at all times. Scriptures reminding us how amazingly he loves us, and how he will never let us go, are easy to find and to meditate upon as we seek out jewels from God's word to ponder each day. Sometimes, though, it's a less obvious verse that leaps out at us. I remember a time of real struggle in my life when my prayers seemed to be bouncing off the ceiling and church meetings left me empty and frustrated. A friend who knew how I was feeling sent me a card with a verse from Lamentations, which has become for me one of my most precious jewels. In Lamentations 2:19 the writer says, 'Pour out your heart like water in the presence of the Lord.' That was what I needed to do! As I came to God and just splurged out what was in my heart (along with the water of many tears), I reconnected with God and worship became a joy once more. That verse has become my favourite definition of prayer and one that I love to share with other people when they are finding it difficult to pray.

I really appreciate Ignatian spirituality and its emphasis on what God's word can say to me in my ordinary everyday situation. I have had the pleasure of attending two Ignatian weekend retreats, and I want to end with something that I felt God saying to me as I packed to leave after an amazing weekend of meeting with him through his word. This is an extract from what I wrote in my journal:

You are amazing, Lord. There was me thinking I was going to have to work so hard to wring something meaningful or relevant from a passage that I had read a hundred times with little inspiration—like getting blood out of a stone—but what happens? Your word springs open like a jack-in-the-box and out spill treasures beyond my wildest dreams. Did I have to mine for them? Was it hard and heavy work? No, these gems were lying there on the surface, sparkling at me, waiting for me to come along and pick them up! I gather them into my lap and sit looking at them, turning them over. Each one is special, each one is different, each one is relevant to a different area of my life. Help me not to lose them on the way home; don't let them roll under the bed when I unpack this evening. Help me not to mislay them as busyness kicks in and silence ebbs away. Let me treasure them, take them somewhere and hide them where only I know where they are. Then next month, when the memory of these days has faded, I can take a moment to go and get them, handle them, see them sparkle and know you speaking these words to me again—words to encourage and strengthen and bring hope; words that remind me of your constant companionship on my journey. Never let me forget that there are always new treasures to find when I take time to turn to you and ask for them. ∎

I take huge reassurance from the fact that God has a purpose for my life

'Pour out your heart like water in the presence of the Lord'

The rock
in times of trouble

Canon Andrew White is President and CEO of the Foundation for Reconciliation in the Middle East (FRME) and the Anglican priest in Iraq. He has written 'Iraq: Searching for Hope' (Continuum, 2005).

Almost every day I am asked how I manage to keep doing what I do. I have been held at gunpoint, beaten, left for hours in rat-infested rooms and much more. Added to this, my health is not good, as I am suffering from MS, and many people would have me put out to grass. I remember, not so long ago, contemplating what I do, while sitting waiting for a military helicopter at the base in the International zone in Baghdad. When we fly in these helicopters, there is no safety briefing. The doors are left wide open and soldiers lean out with their guns targeted. Most times we are shot at, and it takes a little while to get used to the heavenward-directed hostility. I think about the days when I would cycle in my former parish in London; now even the ride around the South Circular would seem totally serene.

I remember my days at theological college and what I was taught there. They did not teach me to write *fatwas* for Islamic clerics or to negotiate for hostages, but they did teach me theology. What's more, they gave me the tools to understand the scriptures. I take out my Bible and it dawns on me that even this book looks different. It is not covered in beautiful black leather with gold-edged pages. No, it's khaki-coloured and its cover reads '3rd Squadron of the 7th Cavalry Regiment'. It's an American military Bible, but in it are the same words that keep me going each day. I open it to Psalm 62 and read, 'He alone is my rock and salvation; he is my fortress,

Andrew with the newly elected Iraqi Prime Minister

I will never be shaken' (vv. 2, 6). Yes, I am surrounded by trouble, yet my God, the God of Abraham, Isaac and Jacob, does not change. He is my rock; he is my security; he is the one I love deeply and he is the one who sustains me even when everything seems to be going against me.

Most of my days are spent in diplomatic and political work. Then there is the highlight of meeting with my people of St George's Church, Baghdad, or in the chapel of Saddam's former palace. Here my congregation is predominantly American. They are living and working in chaos but they also have a total commitment to God

> **We are told to pray for the peace of Jerusalem: we must therefore also work for it**

and to serving his people, despite what the media say.

The following is an account of one recent Sunday in Baghdad. It shows the true nature of our work in Iraq. It shows the true nature of God our rock and salvation, who sees us through even the greatest difficulty—the Creator of the universe, our Lord and our brother.

Sunday in Baghdad

Do you ever have days when you know that God's glory is going to come? Well, today was one of those days.

I started on Saturday night with my security team: 'Tomorrow is a God day, not a political day.' 'Yes, sir,' was the reply.

Early in the morning, we made our way to the Prime Minister's offices—not for politics but for God. It has been decided that it is far too dangerous for me to go to St George's, so we had the service in the Prime Minister's lecture theatre at his invitation. It took the congregation over two hours to enter because of security, but young David took control of the situation and did a great job. (David is the young boy I found, after the war, sleeping by American tanks. He adopted me as his father and now lives at the church.)

My congregation is predominantly American

I spoke of God's glory that I have seen here, glory like in no other place

With my people again, we hugged each other, some cried and then we began. I chose as my text just three words from one of the letters of John: 'God is love'. We had a wonderful service, great singing, OK preaching and tears for Maher, Imman, Yehaya and Firas (the lay leaders of St George's, all killed in September). We talked a lot about them and the mother of Firas was there.

Only the love of Jesus sustains these wonderful people at such a difficult time. As we worshipped, we were joined by several of the Prime Minister's staff, including the Director General, who is a Christian. He pleaded with us to come back. I assured him that while I am in town and can't get to the church, we will be there.

We then had Holy Communion and, as we broke bread, God's glory came. I cannot explain why or what happened, but our Lord was there in power. We then baptized a young child, just 17 days old, called Alexandria. Once again there was great joy, joy that God loved this little girl and us.

Worship in the palace

From the Prime Minister's office we went at full speed to the palace for the service there. As we arrived, mortars came over. The soldiers made us dive for cover and, for a short while, nobody was allowed into the palace. I was actually quite grateful for this, because I was late. This is a far more liturgical service but it has become increasingly free over the months.

There was real joy at the news of the service for the St George's congregation and no concern at all about the recent mortars. This is, after all, the most dangerous parish in the world and here this kind of thing happens all the time.

Here, I am doing a series on people in the Bible who dwelt in Iraq. Today it was the turn of Ezekiel. I spoke of the glory that he saw, and I spoke of God's glory that I have seen here, glory like in no other place. I told people to expect to see God's glory here. I read them part of a recent email from Brett, Alyssa and Emily from All Nations Church in Charlotte, North Carolina, USA. People saw that if these young people can experience the glory of God, surely they could as well.

As I celebrated Holy Communion, God's glory came again. As I looked down from the altar, I could see military officers, with their guns beside them, in tears—tough men with big tears. After the service, person after person came and said that they had seen God's glory in the service. They stayed by me, and we had lunch together and talked more of the glory of God.

In the afternoon, I returned to the Prime Minister's office, where it was announced that the next PM would be Ibrahim Al Jafri, who had won by one vote. I had really wanted Dr Mowaffak, the National Security Adviser, to become Prime Minister, but he did not. I then had some urgent hostage work to do: much of my time in Iraq is spent in delicate hostage negotiations.

Only the love of Jesus sustains these wonderful people at such a difficult time

Alpha Course

This evening we dealt with the subject 'How can we be sure of our faith?' I spoke from 2 Corinthians 5. Once again I read out the email from the girls of All Nations Church as a perfect example of being able to experience God's love. Once again, this was a glorious session when the Lord was truly present. Literally everybody said that it was an amazing and life-changing time. Once again,

13

The founders of Israel referred to their God simply as the Rock of Israel

this was totally because of the Lord and not because of me.

The Alpha course has had an amazing effect here, not just in bringing non-Christians to faith but in encouraging those who already know Jesus. People are truly growing in faith.

Visit to Dr Mowaffak

After Alpha, I called on Dr Mowaffak to make sure he was all right after the appointment of the Prime Minister. He was OK, saying, 'We all prayed to the Lord and he decided it was not for now.' He told me what he wanted me to discuss with the US Ambassador tomorrow. In the evening we will go together to see the Prime Minister.

So this was a Sunday in Baghdad, a day when God's glory has again broken forth. I know now, more than ever, that all things are in the hands of God and he decides. He is indeed our rock and salvation. As I left my security team tonight, they said, 'Today was very different. Something happened to us!'

When we meet with God, we see not only his glory; we see also that he is unmoving, unchanging and all-sustaining. Without him, there is no hope and no future.

From Iraq, I prepare to move to Israel and Palestine. The distance is not far, but from Iraq it is a long journey, involving a helicopter and three planes. Hamas have just been elected as the leaders of the Palestinian Authority. Things are very difficult and very bad, but we in the FRME continue our search for peace. We are told to pray for the peace of Jerusalem: we must therefore also work for it. We travel from Israel to the West Bank and then Gaza, meeting politicians, diplomats and religious leaders. Nobody knows what the future will be, but we still know that God is our rock and he will lead us. We remember that even the founders of Israel were all very secular. They did not want to mention God in their founding document, so they referred to their God simply as the Rock of Israel. This is my God, this is my rock, who enables me to continue the work of the Almighty, come what may. ∎

EDITOR'S NOTE: A VERSION OF THIS ARTICLE APPEARED IN THE MAY 2006 EDITION OF *NEW WINE* MAGAZINE.

The rock

that doesn't roll

Mike Starkey is vicar of Holy Trinity, Twickenham, and a lifelong rock music fan. He has written a number of books, including most recently 'What's Wrong' (2001) and 'Bible Readings for Special Times: Confirmation' (2006) for BRF.

The pun became a Norman trademark

Rarely has a pun generated such excitement and controversy. It gave identity to a whole generation of young Christians, provoked horror and anxiety among an older generation, and married the musical style of the late 1960s, 'rock', with faith in the God of the scriptures, the 'rock' of strength and refuge.

In reality, this was less a marriage of new acquaintances than a reunion after a long separation. The earliest use of the term 'rocking' in popular music was in the black gospel of the southern USA during the first half of the 20th century. Here, rocking meant, essentially, spiritual ecstasy. As early as 1867, the collection *Slave Songs of the United States* contained an early version of the spiritual 'Rock my soul':

Rock o' my soul
in de bosom of Abraham,
Rock o' my soul
in de bosom of Abraham,
Rock o' my soul
in de bosom of Abraham,
Lord, Rock o' my soul.

By the 1940s, the rocking of black church music was borrowed by the mainstream of popular music and divested of its spiritual associations. This was merely the first instance of a process that continues to our day: the passion and energy of black church music being plundered and secularized. The term 'rocking' became a reference to dancing, with a strong sexual subtext. Better known today as rhythm and blues (R&B), it was essentially a secularized version of black church music and, at the time, seldom heard by white audiences.

In 1951, Ohio DJ Alan Freed was the first to play R&B for white audiences, dubbing it 'rock 'n' roll'. By 1956, 'rock 'n' roll' had become a worldwide phenomenon, thanks largely to Elvis Presley. In his legendary Sun Studio recordings of 1954, Elvis covered Roy Brown's 'Good rockin' tonight'. By the release of 'Jailhouse rock' in 1957, the floodgates had opened.

Most churches were horrified, particularly in the US, at the aggression and lewdness of R&B's unruly and illegitimate offspring. For the rest of the 1950s and '60s, rock music and Christian spirituality had little to do with each other, and were often in a state of outright hostility. When British rocker Cliff Richard became a Christian in 1966, his first assumption was that he would have to turn his back on the music that had brought him fame and fortune.

All this began to change in 1969, although the revolution began—as so many revolutions do—almost unnoticed by the general public. Larry David Norman was born in

Rarely has a pun generated such excitement and controversy

1947 in Corpus Christi, Texas but grew up in a black neighbourhood in San Francisco, listening to black church music as well as the rock 'n' roll of the '50s and beat of the '60s. By the late '60s, the neighbouring Haight-Ashbury district of San Francisco had become the global focus for the hippy counterculture.

The young Larry Norman adopted the look of the counterculture, with long hair, jeans and T-shirt. He also adopted the caustic, anti-authoritarian stance of the hippies. But in the case of Norman, a committed Christian formed by the music of black working-class churches, his criticisms

…most churches were not ready for a Christian singer who sounded like Mick Jagger

Norman's achievement was to **reclaim rocking for Jesus** after a long separation

an index finger pointing to heaven. In his 1972 song 'Why should the devil have all the good music?' he sings, 'Jesus is the rock and he rolled my blues away.' On his 1975 album *In Another Land*, Jesus is 'the rock that doesn't roll'. On another Norman standard, 'My Feet are on the Rock', the same pun works overtime: 'My feet are on the rock, my name is on the roll.'

Ironically, *Upon This Rock* is not particularly rocking. Stylistically, it blends the folk-tinged pop of Simon and Garfunkel and the melodic singer-songwriting of contemporaries such as Carole King with elements of black gospel and psychedelia. Later albums would harden the rock edge and the lyrical element of protest, notably 1972's *Only Visiting This Planet*.

Some secular rock critics welcomed Norman's fusion of gospel passion with protest-rock: *Rolling Stone* magazine called Larry Norman 'the most important songwriter since Paul Simon'. Yet album sales remained stubbornly low: most churches were not ready for a Christian singer who sounded like Mick Jagger, had longer hair than their daughters, and sang about drugs and sex.

Eventually, Norman reissued his albums on his own *Solid Rock* record label, and continued to release new material without the help of major labels. These days, anybody wanting

were levelled equally at corporate America and the stuffiness of mainstream religion.

In the late 1960s, Norman was a member of the rock band People!, whose single 'I Love You' reached the US Top 20, but Norman left the band and, in 1969, signed to Capitol Records, recording his first solo album, *Upon This Rock*. The title was a clear reference to both the music he loved and the biblical words of Jesus to Peter: 'On this rock I will build my church, and the gates of Hades will not overcome it' (Matthew 16:18, NIV).

The pun became a Norman trademark, along with his 'One Way: Jesus' badge, with its iconic image of to track down his albums should look in their local Christian bookshop or order direct from his website (www.larrynorman.com). A UK Larry Norman site gives a helpful introduction to the man and his work (www.larrynorman.co.uk).

Norman's lyrics have been controversial. Many of his songs feature apocalyptic visions of the end of the world, and Norman's theology owes a great deal to a questionable 'premillennial' or 'rapture' theology. His song 'I wish we'd all been ready' envisages believers being 'raptured' away from the earth before the return of Christ.

Slowly and surely, however, a revolution had begun. Norman's achievement was to reclaim rocking for Jesus after a long separation. He started a revolution that has transformed the relationship between Christian spirituality and popular culture to this day.

Contemporary Christian Music (CCM) is now a force to be reckoned with. Artists such as Amy Grant, Jars of Clay, POD, Delirious and Switchfoot regularly appear in the secular charts. By 1998, according to *Billboard* magazine, CCM had notched up higher record sales than jazz, classical, New Age and film soundtracks combined. Today's music industry is familiar with the Christian faith of stars such as Cliff Richard, Bono and Daniel Bedingfield. Much of today's church music, particularly youth worship, owes a great deal to the

styles of contemporary rock and dance. Larry Norman himself remains a maverick figure, releasing music via his own website, critical of the big business that has crept into the industry he pioneered and in bad health following major heart surgery in 1992. The revolution he sparked, however, goes from strength to strength.

Even so, doubts remain in the minds of many. Isn't there an unbridgeable gap between the characteristic noise, hedonism and rebellion of rock music and the Christian gospel? Isn't spirituality, by definition,

An important strand of Christian spirituality is celebration

Rocking
meant, essentially, spiritual ecstasy

A key task of the church in every age is **redeeming aspects of the culture**

about meeting with God in the quiet spaces of life? It is true: there is an important spirituality of silence and solitude. But this is only one part of the great tradition of Christian spirituality, and needs to be balanced against other important strands.

A spirituality of celebration.

What is heaven like? According to the book of Revelation, it is a busy city filled with the noise of praise. An important strand of Christian spirituality is celebration. The black churches in particular have valued the role of volume (as opposed to silence), energy (as opposed to calm), and community (as opposed to solitude) as integral to their faith. In a sense, Larry Norman marks the rediscovery by the wider church of its own role in the rise of popular culture, a role that was for a while kept secret both by a godless culture and a fearful church.

The redeeming of culture

When Larry Norman sings 'Why should the devil have all the good music?' he is echoing William Booth of the Salvation Army, who asked in his own day, 'Why should the devil have all the best tunes?' Booth, like the Wesleys before him, was fearless in plundering the popular culture and music of his day. A key task of the church in every age is redeeming aspects of the culture in which it finds itself—taking the best of its art, music and other cultural expressions and using them for the glory of God and enjoyment of people.

There are people in each generation whose calling is to enlarge our vision of spirituality—people who help the rest of us celebrate life and faith, and redeem the culture around us. At the time, they may seem like dangerous radicals and their vision may be misunderstood. All I know is that those Larry Norman albums from the late '60s and early '70s still send a shiver down my spine every time I hear them. ∎

HOPE in a hard place: a true story

With her face pressed up close and eyes turned toward the door, it was almost possible to imagine that the bars didn't exist. Yet a look in any other direction brought her back to reality. At least 30 other cots, all the same—iron bars, thin mattresses, inadequate bedding—formed regimental rows across the room. Like a small rock in a sea of uncertainty, her own familiar bars were a comfort in a curious way, a protection and a demarcation of the space that was hers. Every lump and bump in the mattress was known to her twisted frame, both the ones that caused her pain as she tried to sleep and those that had, over time, moulded to the shape of her body.

Rose fingered a small red plastic cup and saucer. She took pleasure in them—a splash of colour in her monochrome world. She became aware of the noises around her—crying, groaning, sometimes a piercing scream intercepted by shouting. Why did the staff shout so much? Her own voice was rarely heard, yet it served her well if someone rough and uncaring wanted to take her out and bathe her. Her bones were brittle and could easily break. This made the staff fearful to enforce on her what they enforced on others. Her strange

Meryl Leach is married with three children and has lived and worked in West Asia for the past seven years. Meryl trained as a district nurse in London but now she works with her husband to lead a team who are involved in a variety of 'tent making' jobs.

21

Every memory from her eight short years was of a life lived inside these bars

---

at other times there was a softness as the sunlight played among the leaves. This was when she longed to be outside and feel the breeze on her face. Inside it was always the same—the same emptiness and pain. Every memory from her eight short years was of a life lived inside these bars.

Footsteps sounded from the direction of the door. It was too early for food; it must be visitors, Rose thought. She lay quite still, waiting, wanting to notice rather than be noticed. At last they were standing close to her cot, two women and one of the managers. The women were talking to children. Rose held her breath as the younger of the two approached her cot. She had brown hair worn loosely around her shoulders. Her eyes, also brown, were soft and full of life. As she bent, bringing her face level with the mattress, Rose caught a scent of her perfume. The woman smiled at her.

'I'm Elif,' she said. 'What's your name?'

No response. Pointing at the cup and saucer, she asked if they belonged to Rose. Rose kept her silence. For the first time in her life, someone was speaking to her with genuine interest. There must be a catch—Rose would not be fooled.

disease provided a small handle of control in her otherwise dependent existence. Life was a battle and Rose needed every weapon available.

Through the window she could see the distant trees swaying in the breeze. Rose noticed the changes that the seasons brought. Sometimes the trees were stark and bare;

Five years had passed since that day. Elif now stood shivering as the icy wind pushed its freezing fingers inside her coat and chilled her to the core. This unfamiliar place drove her spirits down deeper. She felt numbed by the events of the past few days.

Since that first meeting with Rose, so much had happened. Elif allowed herself to remember their first encounter. She had been working with children for a while and was interested to hear that, after months of trying, permission had been granted to begin volunteer work at a large state orphanage. A few local believers would be paid by a charity to give love and care to the children there. She agreed to visit, believing this was something that God was challenging her to consider.

When she entered the main building for the first time, the stench of vomit and excrement threatened to overwhelm her. Even so, she made her way along the rows of cots and tried to talk to the children. Most seemed to have severe mental and physical disabilities. Some grabbed her, while others just made unintelligible sounds. She wanted to turn and leave.

Then she stopped by a cot with a small girl in it. Big brown eyes seemed to be watching her from a face that gave nothing away. The child's brown hair was cropped short and set her face in an irregular frame. As Elif's eyes moved along the child's body, she noticed that it seemed squashed and twisted. The girl's lower limbs protruded at unnatural angles, and her breathing was shallow and slightly laboured. Elif wondered if the child was in pain. Even though there was no response to the questions she asked, Elif felt that this child had intelligence and she longed to reach her.

As she became a regular visitor to the orphanage, the brown-eyed girl continued to fascinate and challenge her. 'Maybe I can teach her to speak,' she thought. She repeated questions and phrases each time she visited over a number of weeks, but still received no response.

'Goodbye, Rose. See you tomorrow,' she said one afternoon as she prepared to leave. But then illness kept her away, and she was not well enough to return until the following week.

'Morning, Rose,' she greeted the child.

'Why didn't you come back

It was hard to see God as her Father when her earthly father had rejected her

Rose

His love

is the same for each person he has created

last week? You said you would.'

Elif stared at her, shocked. Was it really Rose who had spoken those words? Never had she imagined that she could speak so clearly in such an adult fashion.

The charity gave Rose a wheelchair and she loved to go outside, to revel in the sheer space. Often Elif pushed her just a short distance from the buildings, yet it was away from the noise and confusion and the air smelled fresh. It was out here that she read stories to Rose, stories about Jesus. Rose loved to hear about the things he did and the stories he told. He'd had so much time for those who suffered, the poor, the sick and those tossed upon society's scrap heap. Elif showed her a picture of Jesus bending down to an outcast leper. He was touching the poor bandaged hand and speaking to the man.

One day, Elif put the book down and shared the way in which she had come to find Jesus as more than a story character. She explained the way he had forgiven her and given her a new purpose, and that he was longing for others to respond to his love. She explained that his love is the same for each person he has created, whether they are rich or poor, strong or weak, well or sick. It is a love not dependent on anything a person can do, but a gift to those who would receive and follow.

As Rose began to know Jesus for herself, it was far from easy. There were dark days when she was sullen and angry. It was hard to see God as her Father when her earthly father had rejected her, leaving her in a place where most of the orphans were not true orphans at all, but were rejected disabled people in a society that saw no value, purpose or even humanity in them. Elif encouraged her to bring these feelings to her heavenly Father, to share her needs and hopes and to allow him to be her rock. She prayed together with Elif and the dark clouds would pass.

When volunteers began a feeding programme to supplement some of the children's inadequate diets, Rose was given a 'job'. She was chosen to help a small child named Leah. Elif watched Rose from across the room. First Rose smiled at the solemn figure; Leah looked down, not interested in Rose or the food that she held ready on the end of the spoon. Rose understood: she remembered what it was like to feel sad all the time. With great patience she gently coaxed Leah into accepting one mouthful, then another, until the bowl was empty. With a sense of achievement, Rose looked around and smiled happily as she caught sight of Elif watching her.

Elif had many memories of their friendship together. Rose had taught her so much. Now, though, she could no longer push away the memory of the past few days, of the phone call that had spun her world into chaos. Rose was dead. She had been taken to hospital with a chest infection. Scared and breathless, she was so afraid of the oxygen mask that she refused to wear it. Her frail body couldn't fight back. Her death still didn't seem real, even though Elif had seen her lifeless body.

And here they were now, a small group of Rose's friends, come to remember and to say goodbye. Despite her physical limitations, Rose had had such a strong personality. They gathered around the grave, holding hands as they sang one of Rose's favourite worship songs. Each took a handful of earth and threw it into the grave, thanking God for Rose's short life.

Elif wondered what each of them was remembering. Her own memory made her smile. Months ago, she'd had a dream. She and Rose were somewhere spacious, perhaps a park. The wonderful thing was that Rose was walking beside her, striding along, graceful and confident. Music began to play and Rose started to run, then to dance. It was beautiful to watch. Her hands glided through the air, creating pictures to accompany the music. Her eyes were alive and focused on something or someone beyond where Elif stood, watching, in the dream. Thinking back, she knew now that this dream had become Rose's reality.

The fine dry earth ran through her fingers and tears flowed freely as she whispered goodbye. ∎

> Rose was walking beside her, striding along, **graceful and confident**

With our feet on the Rock

Naomi Starkey is the editor of 'Quiet Spaces'. She also edits 'New Daylight' Bible reading notes, as well as commissioning BRF's range of books for adults.

On Christ the solid Rock I stand, All other ground is sinking sand.

These words formed part of a hymn written by Edward Mote, a London preacher in the 1830s. The words came to him as he walked along Holborn, in central London, and he went on to share them with a friend's terminally ill wife, who found them a great comfort in her final days.

The image of standing on Christ, the one stable point in a mass of quicksand, is a powerful one. It echoes Jesus' parable of 'the wise man who built his house on rock' and the corresponding 'foolish man who built his house on sand' (Matthew 7:24–27; Luke 6:47–49, NIV).

When life takes a wrong turn— anything from losing our front door keys to facing redundancy or worse— we may talk about feeling as if we have 'stepped on a stair that wasn't there' or 'losing our footing'. We may feel as if God has disappeared, as if our faith has evaporated in the crisis we face. And our situation may feel so precarious that we are not so much trying to stand on the rock as scrabble for a toehold on a vertical cliff face.

Yet however desperate we may feel, there are anchor points to hold us to the rock, that we can reach out and grab. Each is different, and may work for us in different ways at different times, yet they all offer a way of keeping ourselves close to God, warmed by his love and sheltered in his care.

The word

Many people describe how familiar, and lesser-known, Bible passages seem to speak to them directly at moments of crisis or periods of ongoing struggle. Prayerful meditation on the Bible, whether via a booklet of daily readings or leafing through a Testament at random, can enable God to bring his word forcefully alive in a situation. As editor of *New Daylight*, I have received many letters from readers telling how a particular day's reading (planned up to two years ahead and written nearly twelve months in advance) has been exactly what they needed.

The Dutch Christian Corrie Ten Boom, arrested with her family for sheltering Jews from Nazi persecution, read the Bible aloud to her fellow prisoners, holding the book in shaking hands because 'so mysterious had it become to me. It was new; it had just been written. I marvelled sometimes that the ink was dry... it was simply a description of the way things were—of hell and heaven, of how men act and how God acts. I had read a thousand times the story of Jesus' arrest—how soldiers had slapped Him, laughed at Him, flogged Him. Now such happenings had faces and voices' (*The Hiding Place*, Hodder, 1972).

On a very different level, a good friend of mine tells how years ago, as a somewhat troubled teenager, she was reading the Psalms in search of help. Struggling with the break-up of a special relationship, overwhelmed

Christ, the one stable point in a mass of quicksand

The church is a body, not a building

by choices about education and the daunting prospect of adult life, she was overwhelmed by this verse from Psalm 119: 'I run in the path of your commands, for you have set my heart free' (v. 32). She knew then that she was in God's presence. He spoke to her and filled her with peace.

The food

We may believe that God is our rock, our source of strength and calm, but if we are full-time carers of small children (for example), we may find that all our usual means of entering God's presence appear closed off. If we can't snatch more than a few

27

...believe that in some way you are encountering the living Saviour

minutes for prayer, go on a quiet day, sit through a sermon or even join in the singing at church, because there is somebody who wants feeding, changing or attention of some kind, what can we do? Are we to stay stranded on the edge, unable even to dip a toe in the spiritual shallows until our infant settles in the crèche (and, like me, you may find yourself waiting indefinitely for that magical day)?

What we can do is—literally—taste and see that God is good. When it is available, take Communion— bread/wafer and wine commemorating Jesus' sacrifice and representing his presence with us (or whichever exact theological slant you put on it)—and believe that in some way you are encountering the living Saviour. Even if you have been out for most of the service, including every word of the

prayers of consecration, you can still come and receive, open to however the Spirit may touch you in the split second before your domestic responsibilities tug on your attention again. That has been my experience over the years, anyway. God is here; his Spirit is with us. Taste and see.

The fellowship

We may feel that our own home church is far from ideal, that it is too dull or too lively or too something-else-not-quite-to-our-taste. Even so, it may be where we believe that God has called us to belong and to worship. It is a truism worth repeating: the church is a body, not a building. If we are part of that body, we will find that fellow members can be a means of blessing to us, as we can be to them.

It is almost unbearably hard if our church situation is actually part of whatever is making our lives difficult. Then we simply have to hold tight to God's hand and ask him to show us the right path to take. On the other hand, if we are blessed with belonging to a caring church community, the memory of that shared fellowship will stay with us and sustain our faith, even if we eventually have to move on.

Take an example: another friend of mine spent years loyally attending the bland, middle-of-the-road church where his family belonged. Intellectual curiosity was discouraged because, as my friend found, when the minister was questioned, he could not defend his own faith on grounds other than those of 'good moral practice'. The general feeling was that it would be preferable to be a Mormon than a Pentecostal (better dressed and less likely to result in embarrassingly enthusiastic religious behaviour).

When my friend went to university, he discovered that church could be different. It could be a place where hard questions were debated and often answered, where services were so packed with young people that they perched on the windowsills, where worship came alive because it was infused with the Holy Spirit and summoned a Saviour whom the congregation believed to be a powerful and present reality.

The memory of that church kept him going through subsequent years of worshipping, and later ministering, in small congregations embroiled in various states of difficulty. He knew from experience that there could be more to church worship and fellowship, that one day there would be more, even if not necessarily in that place at that time.

The cry

We may or may not find consolation in our church community, in the Bible, in the bread and wine—yet we can still cry out to the Lord God for rescue, asking the Rock to deliver us from our rocky time. And it may not be deliverance for ourselves, but for others, or even for a situation that we find God has placed upon our hearts.

I know of an old woman of great faith, who found herself housebound. She knew, though, that God wanted her to pray for the local church—which was not where she had worshipped, partly because she knew it was not only spiritually moribund but notoriously cold in all kinds of ways. She prayed for years, with no sign that anything was happening.

Then, one day, a new minister was appointed and she got the chance to tell him of her burden of intercession for that church. And the church began to change, painfully and tumultuously, but fundamentally. The cry of the faithful prayer warrior had been answered.

Prayerful meditation

can enable God to bring his word forcefully alive

The Rock

We may feel that we are clinging to the rock by a fingernail, that one more blast of the storm will hurl us into the abyss—but we can hold on, if we allow ourselves to be sustained by the care of fellow believers, by God's own word, by the taste of his presence, by knowing that he hears our cry for rescue. And then we may find ourselves able to scramble to our feet, a bit stiff and shaken perhaps, but nonetheless standing upright on the Rock. ■

Let all creation
praise God

(Psalm 148)

This is an abridged extract from 'No Strange Land' by Eddie Askew (The Leprosy Mission International, 1987, 2003). All profits go to support the work of The Leprosy Mission, with whom Eddie and his wife Barbara served for 15 years in India.

I'm sitting at a window in Thimpu, the capital of Bhutan. It's early morning, the air still crisp under a blue sky. Tentative fingers of sunshine stroke the near hills, promising later warmth. Light touches the far mountains. Travelling in Bhutan makes you very conscious of the immensity and power of creation. The enormous forces which thrust up the towering Himalayas, the rush of glacial rivers, moulding smooth the jagged rocks. The continuing processes of growth, erosion still changing the structure and face of the land. Yet these forces of creation are not an end in themselves. They are simply the tools used by God the creator, and the creation is greater than the tools he uses.

Yesterday, we gathered in a small room at a leprosy hospital for a morning communion service... We read Psalm 148—a poem of praise to the creator, the words brought alive by the surroundings. And there we were, ordinary human beings, tapping into the resources and power of this God...

A few days earlier, I'd been in Darjeeling. There, on a clear day, you can see the breathtaking snowy peaks of Kanchenjunga, towering and beautiful. Some days, though, the clouds boil up from the plains below, masking the view. You look out onto grey mist, and it's hard to realize the mountains are still there. But they are. In spite of the mist, they remain just as close, just as real.

So is the presence and power of God. Whether we feel him close, or distanced by our human fallibility, misted by our worries, he is there. His power and love ready to be experienced, lived in, celebrated. ■

I praise you,
Lord of creation.
You spoke the word, and all things came to be.
Lord of life—
You speak the word, and all creation lives,
echoes and shouts with life,
Your life.

No static world, where everything is set in place and nothing moves.
No ancient pile of stones, inert, cathedral quiet,
dozing with old memories, days done.
But full of life, trembling in intensity,
vibrant as quartz crystal,
dynamic with your energy,
power, elemental and profound.
I stand in awe.
All I can do is take my little part in praise with all creation.

Praise and rejoice that this deep power that I call Lord
is crystallised in love,
made personal and close.
The thunder of the universe articulate in quiet voice,
gentle to my ear,
holding itself in readiness to meet my needs.
Lord of the universe, who bends to me,
Creator to created,
Infinite to infinitesimal—
what can I do but praise?

And yet, Lord, pressed by my own busyness and self-created doubts,
I lose my grip on you.
The clouds draw in and shadow me.
The mist wet-blankets me in billows of uncertainty.
My doubt shouts out for reassurance
and comes echoing back, empty handed.
Yet still you're there,
Your presence patient and dependable,
and in its magnet field
I turn again to find you—
true north
by which I orientate my life.

And praise returns.

Music for the soul:

Tu es Petrus

Gordon Giles is vicar of St Mary Magdalene's Church, Enfield, north London. He contributes to BRF's 'New Daylight' notes and has also written 'The Music of Praise' (2002), 'The Harmony of Heaven' (2003) and 'O Come, Emmanuel' (2005) for BRF.

Tu es Petrus, et super hanc petra mea edificabo ecclesiam meam.

You are Peter, and on this rock I will build my Church.

WORDS: MATTHEW 16:18
MUSIC: MAURICE DURUFLÉ (1902–86)

Rock-like, Peter isn't

The French composer Maurice Duruflé is not as well known outside the world of French organ music as he ought to be. On this side of the Channel it is mainly his *Requiem*, completed in 1947, for which he is known. But there is also a little suite of four motets, which are exquisitely beautiful, brief and poignant. Each lasts only a few minutes (and they are often found on recordings of the *Requiem*). These motets are brief anthems intended for use at Communion or as introits at the beginning of a service. They are settings of the Latin texts: *Tota pulchra es*, 'You are all beauty' (Song of Songs 4:7); *Tantum ergo*, 'Therefore we before him bending' (words by St Thomas Aquinas); *Ubi caritas*,

'Where charity and love are found, there God is' (words from the Maundy Thursday footwashing liturgy) and *Tu es Petrus*, 'You are Peter' (Matthew 16:18). Three of these four texts have come to us through Roman Catholic liturgy, but *Tu es Petrus* is a biblical text, often quoted around the time of St Peter's Day (29 June), which is the time when new deacons and priests are ordained in many churches.

We are reminded that Jesus says to Simon, 'You are Peter, and on this rock I will build my church'. Peter, Pierre, Pedro, Pietro, Petrus: the name means 'rock'. For some people, Jesus' statement means, 'Peter, on you I build my church—go to it.' Peter is often portrayed as holding the keys to the kingdom of God, with which to loose and lock, the keys that hold the power of salvation for the future faithful. Peter, some say, is given the power with which to administer Christ's Church on earth. He becomes the first Pope, the first leader, and the Roman Catholic Church does identify itself right back to this moment when Jesus invested his trust in one man. He is also a man who later denied knowing the very one who trusted him. Thus Peter is flawed, and we might find that comforting. Rock-like, Peter isn't, but he is a weak, unreliable human being, like you or me.

We might prefer to notice, as many reformed churches do, that Jesus speaks of building his Church only after Peter has declared that Jesus is the 'Messiah—the Son of the living God'. Thus, for some, the rock or *Petrus* is not Peter himself: the foundation stone is actually the statement of faith in Christ that he makes. The foundation of the Church is not a person but a belief, a faith. It is the belief that another person, Jesus, is God. This is the faith of the Church— that we believe in one God, Father, Son and Holy Spirit. The expression of that faith, by Peter or by anyone else, is the bedrock of our Church.

The composer Maurice Duruflé was a man of faith—a devout Roman Catholic who was organist at the church of St Etienne-du-Mont in Paris from 1930 until his death. He was also Professor of Harmony at the Paris

© Louise Blackmore

There are traditions and truths that remain **strong, like rocks**

Musical Conservatory. He was not a composer who could or would write quickly: he could spend a whole morning writing five bars of music (maybe only a few seconds in duration), only to tear them up in the afternoon. For Duruflé, the creative process was a painstaking, even painful process.

Yet his music is deeply embedded in ancient Christian music and faith. Duruflé turns the ancient into the contemporary, creating a soundworld that is distinctively modern, French and faith-full. It is not just 'modern' music, however: through its textures you can hear the tradition from which it springs. Like looking into a clear pool, you can see not only the pure water, but also the rock below. When you hear Duruflé's music, you can tell that he means it: he believes it, and that cannot be said of all 'religious' music. Underlying Duruflé's musical style is plainsong (Gregorian chant), an ancient, monastic way of singing that is still used today in some churches and cathedrals. For centuries, plainsong was the rock on which all music was built, and scales and 'modes' were devised to give it melodic structure. Even as harmony developed, allowing chords to be created and other melodies to weave independent but connected musical patterns through songs and symphonies, without plainsong much of it would have collapsed. The composer of the past who did not build his music on plainsong was like the man who built his house on sand: it would soon come tumbling down and disappear (see Matthew 7:24–27).

As time went by, musicians abandoned the principles of plainsong and started building works on other foundations. The 20th century was particularly susceptible to this musically atheist trend. Traditional harmony was replaced by apparently more mathematical approaches (Schoenberg and others created 'serial' music, in which every note of the twelve-note chromatic scale would be employed, sometimes with uncomfortable results). But others, like Duruflé, would not abandon the traditions of harmony and

> Duruflé turns the ancient into the contemporary, **creating a soundworld that is distinctively modern**

counterpoint, choosing to remain faithful to what they knew to be true.

Slavish, unquestioning adherence to tradition is not what faith, or music, is about. There are traditions and truths that remain strong, like rocks, on which we can surely stand. If we are grounded on the rock of faith, as so many have been before us, we can explore and be creative and we can be confident and compassionate, trusting always in Jesus Christ, who himself is the true rock of our faith. ■

Music to listen to

'Tu es Petrus' from *Four Motets* by Maurice Duruflé. Available on a CD released by Hyperion (ref: CDA66757) in 1995. Sung by Westminster Cathedral Choir, directed by James O'Donnell.

Readings for reflection

Matthew 16:13–19
Matthew 7:24–27

Pain
in the offering

Wendy Bray is a freelance writer and columnist for a regional daily paper. This extract is taken from the latest updated edition of her book 'In the Palm of God's Hand' (BRF, 2007), chronicling her treatment for Hodgkin's lymphoma and, later, an unrelated breast cancer.

Silence;
hollow yet
howling silence

My haematology consultant tells me it is very unlikely that the lymphoma will return and that I should 'get out there and live life'. With a spring in my proverbial step we go to Spring Harvest at Minehead, where I am on the speaking team. Afterwards, to recover and for a bit of mum/daughter bonding, Lois and I spend a night in Bath, where the scene is set for the next instalment...

Thursday 7 April

Lois and I are at the Ayrlington Hotel in Bath. We spent the day at the Bath Spa Hotel being 'pampered'. Lois loved it—I hated it. I was bored to tears and the massage was agony. Best bit was drinking tea and reading glossy magazines in the lounge after my release.

All this frippery was a prize from *Woman and Home* magazine—a reward for a published letter in which I congratulated them for highlighting the work of the Look Good... Feel Better foundation. I spent a hilarious afternoon in a LGFB group when I had cancer. Seems a long time ago...

Friday 8 April, 7.43am

About half an hour ago, while showering, I leant forward against one arm and felt something odd in my left breast. I felt deep into its depths. It's a hard round area—a huge lump.

I put my head against the tiled wall and wept unbidden, reactive tears as the water cascaded down. I whimpered, 'No, please, no, please, not again.'

The lump is quite large—about 2 inches across—and very hard. How have I missed it?

Lois is still sleeping… she looks so beautiful… my baby, even at 18. Today was supposed to be a happy day, choosing a school prom dress for a beautiful daughter…

Lord?

Evening

Public knowledge tells me that 90 per cent of breast lumps are benign—harmless. Insider knowledge tells me this one isn't. Is that neurosis or experience, Lord?

Yes, it was lymphoma that I had before, not breast cancer, but maybe once you've had cancer you develop a sixth sense—or a sick sense—I'm not sure which. I have spent the day hiding my shock and panic from Lois while shopping, fighting back tears and trying to stay sane.

By lunchtime I decided—as if I had a choice—that the timing just isn't on. Lois has A level exams in a few weeks and Benji has GCSEs. Neither Mum nor Dad is well and Richard is finding work difficult, hundreds of miles away from us.

Lord? I cannot believe that you would allow this. Haven't we had enough?

It's as if the roller coaster has plummeted down the fastest, sheerest slope after the briefest of steady climbs and taken my breath away.

> I put my head against the tiled wall and wept unbidden, reactive tears

> **Lord?**
> I cannot believe that you would allow this

Saturday 9 April

Home. The lump is still there. Oddly, I keep expecting it to disappear.

A miracle seems due. I trawled the internet today for info about it. Big mistake. It could be a cyst or fibro adenoma, but somehow this intruder doesn't exactly fit the description of either. Sounds like a police man-hunt. I'll give it a few days to get lost, and then take it to the surgery if it doesn't—kind of arrest by GP.

I sound lighthearted; I feel desperate. How can the two possibly go together?

Lord, I don't know how to pray or what to pray. I'm incredulous, fearful, lost, maybe even slightly insane with disbelief.

> **I sound lighthearted; I feel desperate.** How can the two possibly go together?

Monday 11 April

Richard's birthday. I still haven't told him. Can't see the point until I know for sure. I'm just glad that he's in London this week and didn't pick up my angst over the weekend. No GP appointments left today—will have to ring again tomorrow.

Evening

Driving back from Tesco today, I was wondering if it's best to ignore it and hope it will go away, at least until after the children's exams. How can I do this to them?

Strangely, I feel as if I knew something like this was coming, but I'd dismissed it as neurosis. It's so easy to believe that the worst will always happen.

Broke the small, brown Hornsea pottery vinegar pot that Mum gave me when I went off to college. It was so precious, but it flew out of the pull-out larder and smashed on the floor. I wept. Crying over spilt vinegar? Or broken dreams?

Lord? You're silent. Isn't there anything to say?
Sometimes I wonder why I ask. I know you're there—I have known your love and faithfulness. It's just that you

seem to have deserted me right now. Last time around, there was so much dialogue: I would ask and you would answer. And this time? Silence; hollow yet howling silence.

Sobbed in the bath tonight. Could hardly speak to R on the phone. He must think me very odd.

I am begging you to take this away, Lord, because if this is cancer and the lump is this huge, I must be in big trouble. My books talk about lumps of 1 and 2cm—this is the size of a large pickled onion, and it seems to have come from nowhere.
   Lord, please give me your peace. Speak to me, reassure me. I am terrified.

Tuesday 12 April

It's 6.15am and I have just made a cup of tea. I'm sitting up in bed to do my Bible reading and pray, rather than toss and turn with worry. Somehow I've got to ring the GP's surgery bang on the dot of 8am (as required by the system) without the children knowing. Yet that's just the time they are leaving for school, and if I leave it even ten minutes all the appointments for today will be gone again.

Evening

By stealth and sleight of hand I managed to get a GP appointment for this morning.
   'Blimmin' 'eck,' said my GP. I think that's medical speak for 'There is some cause for concern here.' Funny that. Something in me felt sure he'd say, 'Oh! Aren't you lucky to have one of these? Don't shout about it or everyone will want one and I'll be inundated!'
   He was brilliant actually—as ever. No faffing, no fuss, just good humour, expertise and action. 'I'll phone the hospital straight away,' said he. 'With your history we can't be too careful.' Why, when someone says 'with your history', do I always feel antique with the patina to prove it? And why did it worry me that he was dialling the hospital as I left the room?
   It'll be OK... It will be OK—won't it? ■

I am begging you to take this away, Lord...

Lord, please give me your peace. Speak to me, reassure me. I am terrified

Condensed Church

Nick Flint grew up in Sussex and has ministered to parishes in the diocese of Chichester since being ordained in 1987, working since 1996 in his current post at Rusper and Colgate. An amateur family historian, he made the surprising discovery that he is related to most of his predecessors at Rusper between the years 1590 and 1890.

The Church is formed like igneous rock

Most of us are still 'green' in faith terms

The challenge for our congregation was to bring the liturgical year to life. The reason, to coin a phrase, was 'Because it's there!'—so much a part of the Christian landscape as to risk being taken for granted by those who have travelled it so many times, or equally unappreciated by those new to 'the Way'. A ready-made visual aid, which came to hand from our Anglican tradition, was in the form of the different colours in church clothing and furnishings. These tell the worshipper at a glance whether we are in a season of penitence (purple), celebration (gold/white), 'ordinary time' (green) or marking Pentecost or the feast of a martyr (red).

The Sunday assembly should surely be an expression of the summit of our worship, so why not choose an ordinary Sunday to take a journey in prayer and song through the whole Church year? Thus the idea of 'CondensedChurch' was born. It was aimed primarily as an amnesty for those not seen at church lately—not to weigh them down with guilt, but to cajole them gently with cartoons and reel them in with refreshments. In the united parishes of Rusper and Colgate, north of the rolling Sussex Downs in the diocese of Chichester, the congregation chose to take just such an otherwise undesignated, ordinary last Sunday of May as an opportunity for experienced climbers and newcomers alike to gain a new perspective on this ascent. The Christian journey, however well trodden, is thankfully never just a matter of simply getting from A to B by the shortest route. We promised not to linger in Lent and scarcely to pause for Pentecost, but to career towards Christmas and tear through Trinitytide. And this service proved a surprisingly moving experience for all who took part.

Hills of the north, rejoice!

Advent recalls the equivalent, in liturgical time, of the geological periods when sedimentary rock was slowly being laid down. Consolidation over long centuries gained the people of God a growing sense of their identity while building our Old Testament foundation. Like particles of older rock, elements of the personal and inherited past shape the 'now' of the Advent experience. We followed John the Leveller's pointing finger (see Luke 3:1–6) across mountain and valley to the distant horizon.

The experience of celebrating the next step of the journey by carol singing was a new one for most of us

Elements of the personal and inherited past shape the 'now' of the Advent experience

in May! From the vantage point of Christmas, with the priest suitably attired in a white stole, we looked down, as it were, on the nations spread out before us awaiting their

Even Moses and Elijah were both brought down to earth again after their mountain-top experiences

emerged into the stark landscape of Calvary. Holy Week is like the sudden extreme in which metamorphic rock is created. From the moment when Jesus warns the religious leaders that the rocks will cry out if his disciples are silenced (Luke 19:40), the Gospels themselves do not hesitate to describe the events of the cross and resurrection in graphic terms of rock-splitting phenomena (Matthew 27:51; 28:2).

Epiphany. This was not, however, to be the usual leisurely twelve-month amble through the year. Aiming to finish the service as promised, within the hour, the priest now hastily donned his purple stole once more, inviting us to scramble up the suddenly steepening slope of the penitential season, the bare rocks of Lent making confession a firm foothold.

But the steep and rugged pathway may we tread rejoicingly

The paschal passage, which we next entered, was a narrowing and darkening one, from which we

There is a green hill far away

From that green hill we trudged up the Emmaus road before running back down the same path, singing our 'Alleluias' on the way to the empty cave tomb. Hardly pausing for breath, we were caught up in Pentecost, that volcanic moment when the Holy Spirit, always present but hidden under the surface, bursts forth and nothing is ever the same again. The Church is formed like igneous rock, and no sooner constituted than tested by blood and fire. Yet from the rocks like those that crushed Stephen (Acts 7:59), the first martyr, the Church is constantly being rebuilt into a living temple.

He makes me down to lie in pastures green

The Trinity season affords a gentler, more pastoral aspect, with its shades of green rounded hills and valleys and the good shepherd as our guide—a familiar landscape to a congregation in south-east England. This season covers the yearly stretch of the calendar through summer and autumn. The colour green, meanwhile, reminds us that we have much to learn: most of us are still 'green' in faith terms! We subtitled this stage of the service 'Life in God', with the focus more on our personal pilgrimage as Christians than on tracing the steps of Jesus' life and ministry, as we usually do in the months between Christmas and Pentecost.

Lush green also suggests a spiritual rain pouring from clouds of glory, clouds of witnesses, reminding us of the calling of the saints in every age. Saints' days pop up in the calendar at regular intervals, rather like glimpsing a sherpa or experienced mountaineer on the path ahead, to encourage us. One of our churches is dedicated to Mary Magdalene, while other saints with significance for the parishes are Benedict and Francis. From a distance, there may appear to be a yawning chasm between such holy people and ourselves. We might do well, then, to pause and remember how even Moses and Elijah were both brought down to earth again after their mountain-top experiences, before sharing in Christ's transfiguration (see Exodus 32; 1 Kings 19:10; Matthew 17:1–8; Mark 9:2–8; Luke 9:28–36).

This familiar journey through the Christian year is full of surprises. We may be familiar with the idea that a liturgical year begins in Advent, but it does not seem to have a recognized ending; instead the cycle repeats itself. So where and how was our service to reflect this? The mountain-top experience that suggested itself was that of the crew and passengers of Noah's Ark on Ararat as the waters

This familiar journey
through the Christian year is full of surprises

receded—a new beginning if ever there was one! To reflect this event, we reaffirmed our covenant relationship with God and dedicated ourselves anew to our baptismal calling in the words of the following prayer. ■

PRAYER

Give us vision, courage and joy and make us one, that the world may believe that Jesus is Lord, to your eternal glory. Amen

Foundations
for change

Bruce Stanley is a life coach, spiritual director and trainer. He can be found at www.brucestanley.co.uk.

> **The most effortless change happens when we are in harmony**

Anything is possible, especially when we're prompted to change by the Holy Spirit

I remember, as a young boy, the enjoyment of swimming underwater. I wasn't much good on the surface (my stationary breaststroke is still a marvel), but underwater I was in my element. I remember especially the sensation of sliding down the side of the pool, deep underwater, with my knees pulled up to my chest, and then pushing against the wall and gliding for a width or more. Without the wall, progress was much harder.

There are similar principles involved in making changes in our lives, especially when those changes involve a certain degree of internal challenge. The most effortless change happens when we are in harmony: when our opportunity, capability, will and actions are all in line. Then, some would say, anything is possible, especially when we're prompted to change by the Holy Spirit and we find God's resources enabling our journey. The part of the equation that is often missing, though, is our will. Without that internal alignment, change will be difficult.

The substrata

So where is the rock inside on which to build, change, undertake challenge or overcome difficulty? What is this internal structure made up of? What are its different levels?

At the surface, there is our behaviour: what we do, how we react, our actions. These are often what we want to change. Remember Paul saying, 'For what I want to do I do not do, but what I hate I do' (Romans 7:15, NIV)? If we believe that we are what we do, then this will be where we notice (or others point out) things that we wish were different. It could be something as obvious as smoking or eating habits, or anger, or our speech or health that we want to change. Our behaviour also describes how hard we try when faced with a challenge, how often we give something a go if the going is tough, whether we smile at strangers or avoid eye contact when we're out and about. It is where we meet the world. Many of the verbs we can think of are about our surface behaviour: acting, building, collecting, discussing, embracing—the alphabet goes on.

It is at this level that we often desire change, but all our behaviour is simply following the guiding instruction of the next level down: our beliefs, values and conditioning. This might be the right place to look for our conflicting 'spiritual' and 'worldly' natures, to continue with Paul's description.

Most New Year resolutions are a battle between our determination and our behaviour. Which normally wins for you? For most of us, it is our behaviour. Our automatic path of least resistance is for behaviour to follow beliefs, and this is where real change begins. It is understanding this level of ourselves, and planning change informed by our understanding, that leads to harmonious and resistance-free progress. Deeper even than our beliefs lies a further layer, which I'll explore at the end.

Values

A key part of this middle layer of beliefs and conditioning are our values: the rules that direct our automatic behaviour. What are the values that govern our behaviour as an employee, parent or marriage partner? What values instruct our behaviour when

At the surface, there is our behaviour: what we do, how we react, our actions

We need to find stillness

Asking ourselves 'why?' will lead us to our values

we're unfairly criticized or about to be interviewed for the 14th job in a row? What are the values that mean we are angered within seconds of hearing some news story, or delighted by something that happened yesterday? What do we say without even thinking when someone bumps into us on the street?

Asking ourselves 'why?' will lead us to our values. We can also ask others to suggest what they think our governing rules are. If we end up with a glowing list of delightful and inspiring words, then we might not have done the work accurately! Being right, having the last word, needing the positive affirmation of others or feeling comfortable in the role of victim are all very common values that crop up in these exercises, as much as do loving creativity, sharing with others, increasing happiness and promoting peace. It is vital to be honest.

Identifying our core values can help us to know how best to undertake activities, especially if we are trying to do something differently. If we plan actions in line with our values, we meet less resistance, whether those values are glowingly wonderful or rather compromised. Decision-making is a good example. Are you a 'maximizer', who needs to have seen every possible choice, or somebody for whom the first good match will do? If there are two of you involved in making a decision, it is vital to be clear about the values that influence each one of you.

Motivation

Closely related to values—the internal rules that we follow when we act in a particular way—there is motivation, which could be described as the reasons why we act in a particular way.1

Motivation as a subject relating to change can cover the driving forces giving rise to the desire to change in the first place—what we might be wanting to move away from or move towards. These forces can describe which parts of a project we like: the instigation, the building or the finished product. Motivation also influences how we interrelate with others. Are you people-focused or task-focused?

Think back to projects and activities that you felt showed you at your best and see what patterns emerge. Do you pursue pleasure or avoid pain? Do you rely on external rewards to get things done? Are you numerically motivated—do you find it easier to get a job done when you break it into measurable steps? Whatever picture emerges, one important tip is that motivation follows action, not the other way round. Get past the inertia of inaction and then motivation will follow.

Motivation and values are our 'wall to push off' if we want projects or change to happen easily and efficiently. But they are not the hardest, firmest part of us. They are not the changeless substrata of rock. Finding this is the real key to change, which can seem contradictory when we consider that it is the most elusive part of us—our being, our spirit.

All our behaviour is simply following the guiding instruction of the next level down

Get past the inertia of inaction and then motivation will follow

Moulding clay

It is very good news that our middle layer of beliefs, conditioning, values and motivations aren't actually 'set in stone'. They are more like clay. They are mouldable. How would you prefer to behave in the future? How would you like to react to challenges? How would you like to be towards others? With all these things, we are clay, not rock.

Think about some situation that really pushes you beyond your comfort zone. What is it that disturbs your sleep? Well, it isn't the event itself that disturbs you; it is your beliefs about the event—your interpretation of it. A good example might be an interview for a job: you've been to 14 interviews already and you're filled with dread about the one coming up in ten days' time. Dread is the behaviour, the symptom you most notice. It is what is happening on the surface, and this is where you might try to bring about change. 'Stop worrying,' you tell yourself, or you might take sleeping pills or pray or try to deal with the symptoms in other ways.

In fact, you should be looking at the real cause. What do you believe about the interview that is giving rise to this behaviour? If you could uncover these beliefs, you might be able to replace them with beliefs of your choosing that would give rise to different behaviour—no worrying and a confident interview. With some dedication, it can be as easy as that. I have seen someone give up smoking effortlessly by first listing the five beliefs, off the top of his head, that he felt gave rise to his behaviour, and then devising five beliefs that would support his preferred behaviour of not smoking. Ask God to inspire your reflections and, when you have some new intentions, pin them up or write them out 15 times.

The paradox of being

So what is the bit of us that is rock, the part that doesn't change? Knowing this 'being' part of us creates a wider awareness and acceptance, which means that change in our beliefs and behaviour can happen painlessly. From the solid perspective of our essential inner being, we are freed from the identification with the problem that we are hoping to change. Instead of 'me' changing 'me', a distinction appears. Try simply observing yourself without labelling or judgment, and remember to think, 'This is in me; it doesn't define me.'

For example, if my issue is lack of confidence, and if I define myself by what I do, then I would say that 'I am unconfident'. There isn't anything else left free from that feeling because I've decided that 'I am' it. But if I have a glimmer that I am more than just my beliefs and behaviour—if I have a sense of being that encompasses the rest—then I would say, 'There is a lack of confidence in me', which means that there might be some resources left over for effecting change. It could even be that I'm happy to accept the feeling and carry on regardless: the feeling might then just lose power on its own. Paradoxically, the more we can accept the present moment from this perspective, the more easily change happens.

Most importantly, we need to find stillness. By shifting focus from whatever problem seems set in stone, we will find that we and God's Spirit who fashioned us are more solid than the ground we walk on, a position from which it is much easier to change. Knowing that we are part of God and made in God's image envelops us in creative examples of harmonious, enriching growth. In the words of Isaiah 51:1, 'Look to the rock from which you were cut and to the quarry from which you were hewn.' ■

Think about some situation that really **pushes you beyond your comfort zone**

... change in our beliefs and behaviour can happen painlessly

Clare
of Assisi

a strong woman

Helen Julian CSF is an Anglican Franciscan sister, a member of the Community of St Francis and presently serving the community as Ministry Provincial. She contributes to 'New Daylight' and has also written 'Living the Gospel', 'The Lindisfarne Icon' and 'The Road to Emmaus' for BRF.

Every house of Franciscan sisters or brothers that I've ever known has had a copy of the San Damiano crucifix, usually in a prominent place in the chapel. This beautiful icon of the crucified Christ links the two founders of the Franciscan way, Francis and Clare.

Clare also came from Assisi in central Italy, and was born in the last decade of the twelfth century, about eleven years after Francis. She came from an aristocratic family, unlike Francis, who was the son of a cloth merchant. After trying and failing to become a knight, Francis had a series of conversion experiences, which led to his adopting a radically different form of life, committed to poverty and to preaching the gospel. One of the most striking of these experiences took place in the tiny tumbledown church of San Damiano, where he was praying in front of the crucifix, asking

God what he wanted him to do. He thought he heard the crucifix speak to him: 'Francis, go and rebuild my church, which, as you see, is falling down.' Francis took the command literally, and rebuilt San Damiano and other churches before realizing that God had a much bigger task in mind.

So he began to preach in the squares of Assisi, and it was here that Clare heard him and was captivated by his vision of living the gospel life. She met Francis in secret, accompanied only by a friend. Finally, on Palm Sunday 1212, aged 18, she left home in the middle of the night to join Francis in his radical life. He and the few men who had already joined him met Clare, who laid aside her fine dress and was clothed in a simple habit. Francis cut her hair, and she promised obedience to him.

Clare always saw Francis as the inspiration of her vocation, but she was also a strong woman in her own right. When she left home, she had no idea where she would be living or who would be with her. Unlike the men who came to join Francis in the early days, she had no community to join. Initially Francis took her to a nearby Benedictine convent, but soon it was clear that she could not live there the way of life to which she and Francis were both called. Clare came to live at San Damiano, where Francis had heard the crucifix speak. One of her own sisters came to join her there, followed by many other women including several further members of her family, and the community of the Poor Clares

Clare heard him and was captivated by his vision of living the gospel life

Clare always saw Francis as the inspiration of her vocation

(as they are now called) had come into being.

Although Francis probably spent a lot of time with Clare and her sisters in the early days, as his own community grew he visited less and less frequently, and Clare had to find her own path. She became Abbess at San Damiano, much against her will, in 1215, and remained so until her death in 1253. Francis himself died in 1226, and Clare became one of the main defenders of the poverty he had so much valued. Even before Francis' death, she had already begun her own battle with those in power in the church, who wanted the sisters to have property and money to secure their safety and livelihood. Clare instead sought 'the privilege of poverty', and defended it against even the Pope, who offered to

Clare had gradually to turn to Christ as the inspiration of her life

absolve her from her vow.

Clare had gradually to turn to Christ as the inspiration of her life, rather than to Francis, and in this she must have been helped by the long hours of prayer that she spent before the crucifix at San Damiano. In several letters that she sent to Agnes, the abbess of a Poor Clare community in Prague, she writes glowingly of Christ as the centre of the life of prayer that she embraced, encouraging Agnes to gaze on him as she herself surely did. 'Love him totally who gave himself totally for your love,' she writes.

Even during Francis' lifetime, their relationship had become more equal than Clare's vow of obedience would suggest. When he was perplexed about his own vocation, Francis consulted Clare and one of his brothers, Sylvester, about whether he should continue to preach or give himself entirely to prayer. He sent one of his brothers to Clare for healing and, in his final illness, came to San Damiano, where Clare cared for him.

Francis had written a brief Rule for the sisters; Clare spent her whole life struggling to get a Franciscan Rule, including Francis' words, approved for her community. Finally, in 1253, Clare's own Rule, the first to be written by a woman, was approved by the Pope. The precious document was taken to Clare, already gravely ill, and she kissed it lovingly. The next day, 11 August, she died. The Pope tried to declare her a saint on the day of her funeral and, being thwarted in this, began the process of her canonization less than two months after her death. She was declared a saint in 1255.

'The Son of God became for us the Way, which Francis has shown and taught us by word and example,' Clare wrote near the end of her life. Inspired by Francis initially, she came to find her own way, centred on Christ, and became a strong rock to many of Francis' other followers after his death. ∎

Through the Valley of Rocks

'Are we nearly there yet? How much further is it?' Which of us parents hasn't heard these questions from our children, probably only three miles into a 300-mile journey? When it comes to approaching Lee Abbey in north Devon, anyone who has not visited before could be forgiven for asking those two questions. The conference, retreat and holiday centre is located in a spectacular environment where Exmoor meets the sea but, sadly, Exmoor does not do so conveniently near the M5.

Having finally arrived at the twin villages of Lynton and Lynmouth, the visitor to Lee Abbey drives through the Valley of Rocks, whose rock formations make a striking entranceway to our estate. Many guests say that even if they have not stayed at Lee Abbey before, they have seen this natural wonder as they

... to build community

Chris Edmondson has been Warden of Lee Abbey since 2002. Before that, he worked as Diocesan Missioner in Carlisle Diocese and then Vicar of St Peter's Shipley in the Diocese of Bradford. He is author of a number of books, including 'Fit to Lead' (DLT, 2002) and 'Fit for Community' (DLT, 2006). He is married to Susan and they have two grown-up sons.

have passed through the area. This is where the 'wow' factor sets in and that long journey feels worthwhile.

The journey of faith that established the place has been equally exciting and certainly worthwhile. Most of the main

... equally exciting and certainly worthwhile

house at Lee Abbey was completed in the mid-19th century, although older origins are indicated by the sundial in the central courtyard, dated 1650. Different generations of the Bailey family who owned the estate have made their own contributions, not least 'Squire' Bailey, who, before his death in 1921, was responsible for much of the tree-planting and landscaping of the estate. After his death, the estate was sold and the house and 300 acres were bought by a hotel company.

The hotel era lasted for 15 years from 1924, and during this time the south wing and dining room were added, along with many more bedrooms. The Beach Chalet was also built at this time, initially as a café but now enjoyed as a self-catering unit for up to twelve people, with an amazing view over Lee Abbey's beach. But, as we know, the 1930s saw the Depression, and the hotel companies that ran Lee Abbey both went bankrupt in 1939.

During the closing years of World War II, a number of men already involved in Christian holiday ventures with young people were looking for a more permanent centre for that kind of ministry, and Lee Abbey seemed an ideal location. At the time, a boys' school evacuated from London had taken over the place, but during the school summer holidays of 1943, Roger de Pemberton, who would become the first Warden of Lee Abbey, ran a house party on the site.

Over a cup of coffee at the Tea Cottage (which still operates in the summer holiday weeks), Roger shared his vision with one of his house party team. The scheme was very simple: he wanted to buy Lee Abbey as a centre for evangelism and lay training. In the same year, the Archbishop of Canterbury, William Temple, had commissioned a report called 'Towards the conversion of England'. Temple had a passion to address the spiritual poverty of the Church of England, which had been revealed in the war years. Roger was a key member of the Archbishop's group, which longed to address the 'wholesale drift from organized religion'. The report also recognized the need to mobilize and train lay people if this task of evangelism was to be fulfilled effectively. Could Lee Abbey be part of the answer to this challenge?

It was evident that once the war ended, the school would leave, making the house and estate available for purchase. Neither Roger nor others who shared his vision had any money. However, as he continued to pursue what to many seemed a foolhardy scheme, a group of people came together to pray and discover whether or not the hand of God might be on this 'venture of faith'.

Cutting a long story short (read *The Lee Abbey Story* by Richard More for a detailed account), the group stepped out in faith and made the commitment to purchase Lee Abbey. Only then (and this has so often been the case since) did the money start to appear. In this instance, Roger heard that he had been left an unexpected legacy of £6000, a great deal of money in 1945. He offered this as a loan for the mortgage down-payment. The total cost of purchase was £28,000.

On Michaelmas Day 1945, Roger and the group took over the house with a view to using it as a permanent centre for house parties, retreats and conferences, where people of all ages and backgrounds could think through together the true meaning of the Christian life. They could then return to their homes, places of work and churches, refreshed and renewed in body, mind and spirit, with a better understanding of faith and a deeper commitment to living and sharing it.

Although the world is a very different place 60 years on, and a huge amount of

_____

... to play a distinctive part in **renewing and serving the church in our own generation**

_____

... to be God's welcome to the thousands of people who come to Devon each year

development and improvement work has taken place on site, the essential vision that captured Roger de Pemberton and his group remains at the heart of what Lee Abbey is and does.

That vision has three key

elements—first of all, to play a distinctive part in renewing and serving the church in our own generation. We are continually bombarded with depressing headlines that reflect the decline in numbers and influence of the church in the United Kingdom. The issues that concerned William Temple and others in the 1940s are even more stark in the early years of the 21st century.

Through the ministry at Lee Abbey itself, through taking a team to a church or group of churches, through Household Communities currently operating in Blackburn, Birmingham and Bristol, and through the International Students' Club in central London, the aim is to bring women, men, young people

... a new or renewed encounter with the living Lord Jesus Christ

and children to a new or renewed encounter with the living Lord Jesus Christ. The result of this is enabling and encouraging them to serve God in today's world through the power of his Spirit.

As the second key element in its vision, through the varied year-round programme and commitment to hospitality, Lee Abbey aims to be God's welcome to the thousands of people who come to Devon each year. It's a frenetic, often stress-filled world, and many people are looking for 'quiet spaces'. There are a number of midweek and weekend opportunities for retreat.

Lee Abbey also seeks to be a resource for individual guests and church groups, in areas of healing and wholeness, environmental issues, learning more about how to be a church shaped by and for mission, Bible teaching, performing and creative arts, or input especially for leaders on leadership and vision. Equally, at almost any time of the year, people can come and simply 'chill out' in the space and beauty of the house and grounds. Many people find healing and restored hope in this 'spacious place' (Psalm 18:19).

A concern for young people has always been at the heart of Lee Abbey's ministry. A regular programme for children and young people runs in the main house, plus four weeks of youth camps in the summer. But an exciting new dimension to the ministry, since 2004, is the Beacon Youth and Outdoor Centre. This facility especially welcomes school and youth

groups, Christian and non-Christian, who enjoy not just the location but also activities such as indoor wall-climbing, archery, low ropes, pond dipping and orienteering. There are also some specialist weeks and weekends, such as 'Dads and Lads' and 'Really Wild Weeks' (for details, see www. TheBeaconYouthCentre.org.uk).

The third and final part of the Lee Abbey vision is to build community. From the beginning, there has never been a paid staff, but a community, taking inspiration from the values found in Acts 2:42–47, along with examples of intentional community that have emerged down the centuries of Christian history.

At the time of writing, the community is made up of 20 different nationalities: single people, couples and families called by God for a shorter or longer period to what we describe as 'the costly adventure of community living'. While Lee Abbey has an Anglican foundation, it is interdenominational as well as international, giving a unique opportunity of forming and shaping for God's work, both here and as people move on from Lee Abbey. For many guests, it is sharing in the life of this community that makes the visiting experience so special. ■

Come and simply 'chill out' in the space and beauty of the house and grounds

The rock

These prayers are written by Janet Lancefield, who is a member of Middlesbrough Baptist Church and is married with two daughters. She teaches social work at the University of Teesside and has been a freelance writer for many years.

Among the rich images in the Bible, 'rock' is used in several different contexts. Each prayer will seek to address one of these ideas. All scripture quotations are from the New International Version.

Sunday

'On this rock I will build my church' (Matthew 16:18).

Loving God, Creator of all that is good, thank you for establishing your Church, not on shifting sands or in slippery mud but on a rock. May I recognize the firm foundation and cling to that rock, to your Church, which you love.

As the waves of human irritations and worldly worries surround me, may I be set free to worship you in your Church, loving those who are in fellowship with me. And amid all the trappings of what our human minds conceive as worship, may we find you, the bedrock of our souls. Amen.

Monday

'Strike the rock, and water will come out' (Exodus 17:6).

Lord of hopeless situations, may I believe in your promise to be more than I can ask or think. In your wisdom, help me to believe that a miracle can occur, even when there seems to be no answer to my call.

In the hardness of some situations, in the barrenness of lost hope, help me to trust that you will provide refreshment, living water and healing. Amen.

Tuesday

He will… set me high upon a rock (Psalm 27:5).

Thank you, Lord, that you lift me up and set me high upon a rock, so that I might see behind and peer ahead and, just for an instant, view life from a higher plane. Free me from the everyday, and lift my eyes to the hills, which remind me of your presence.

May I view earth from heaven's perspective; may I see the bigger picture, the longer view, as I continue to rejoice in you. Amen.

Wednesday

… in the clefts of the rock, in the hiding places on the mountainside (Song of Songs 2:14).
Be my rock of refuge, to which I can always go (Psalm 71:3).

Sometimes, Lord, I need to step aside from the daily rush and find new strength from you. You give me shelter in the safety of your presence, where I may hide and think and pray.

I look out from the cleft, waiting for the time when I feel ready to enter the busyness of my life again, renewed by my powerful Rock. Amen.

Thursday

Who is the Rock except our God? (2 Samuel 22:32).
You have not remembered the Rock, your fortress (Isaiah 17:10).

Lord God, my Rock and my fortress, I put my faith in a pebble; it slipped. I tested the scree; it moved. I held on to a branch; it swayed, and then snapped. I reached for long strong grasses; I could not grip. Only my Rock was secure and firm; nothing else would do.

Lord, as I reach out and hold on to different things, remind me: you alone are my Rock—my sure foothold. Amen.

Friday

'It had its foundation on the rock' (Matthew 7:25).

Keep my foundations secure, Lord, so that my house may not crumble or be blown down by a winter storm, or swept away by a rising tide. Shore me up when I need it, by your word, by your power, by your people.

Show me how I can provide shelter for others, a place of security when they are struggling, and give me the grace to lean on others when I find myself sliding. Amen.

Saturday

'There is no one holy like the Lord; there is no one besides you; there is no Rock like our God' (1 Samuel 2:2).

Holy Lord, God of security and safety, when I'm on the rocks, lead me to you, the Rock. When I'm thirsty and the heat's too much, may I drink the living water that you provide and seek the shelter of your shadow. When I need to hide, be my place of refuge.

Lift my feet out of the sand, the mud, the clay. I praise you because nothing but you, the true Rock, will keep me safe. Amen.

Turnstones

Momentarily summer:
a full flowering in a flutter
of white-barred wings, scatter-
ing the darkness in lifting limpet light.

My head is down in the rain
(my friend is dying). Turn-
stones going about their business,
alarmed at my intrusion,

summon me to heaven.

BARRIE ARMSTRONG

Musings of a middle-aged mystic

Veronica Zundel is a journalist, author and contributor to 'New Daylight'. She has also written 'The Time of Our Lives' for BRF. She lives in north London.

Nearly 35 years ago, in the middle of a small party in a friend's college room, I lay down on the floor and refused to move a muscle. I honestly thought I would never move again, and that I would be left to die there. As it happened, within minutes a friend got me up by the creative move of tickling my feet. For the next few days, however, I was alternately withdrawn and furious, until the quiet presence of friends around me restored me to normality.

This was my first encounter with the depression that is still intermittently my companion all these years later. The reason I am writing about it now is that while I lay on that floor, feeling as though I'd reached rock bottom, that was exactly what I felt there: rock. Not just the floor under me, but something deeper—a foundation supporting me, below which I could not fall. Something ancient, solid, on which I could rest and be held up.

'Rock' is one of those biblical images of God that crops up (pun intended!) in hymns and choruses occasionally, yet is rarely explored at any depth. Perhaps we are nervous of the escapist spirituality of 'Rock of ages, cleft for me, let me hide myself in thee', fearing that images of hiding in a cave might lead us into an 'other-

Something ancient, solid, on which I could rest

> That rock has a way of turning up again **when we reach rock bottom**

worldly' faith that is no earthly use.

Yet rock is a central image of God in the Bible, from Genesis onward. So what did it mean to the Bible's first writers and readers, and what might it mean to us now?

Clearly it is an image of strength— something that does not break. It is also a picture of shelter: in a sunbaked desert, you can hide behind a rock and get shade (and even in some cases, as Moses demonstrated, water). A rock is not easily moved; it does not sway with the wind or wear away in one sandstorm. It is also, of course, something we can build with, and Jesus (who, as a carpenter, probably knew a bit about building) pointed out that it was the best thing to build *on*, too. People could be rocks: Simon, the most rash and unreliable of the apostles, was still in Jesus' eyes Peter, the rock, on whom the Church would be built. Indeed, his memories and understanding became central to the vulnerable new movement.

Today, we still talk about people as being rocks—for instance, 'X was a rock of strength for me when my parents died'—and medieval castles stand around our country as a reminder of how a fortress built on rock can defend many people against attack. Many of us have our special places—a rocky cove, a stonebuilt manor house—that speak to us of the enduring, protective power of rock. Personally, I've always loved caves and underground passages. Somehow, entering into the heart of a rocky mountain gives me a great sense of security, and yet also a sense of awe and mystery.

Does rock, however, conjure up for you something hard, unyielding, unable to sympathize with human feelings? God is not 'stony-faced', but is that paradox, a 'living rock' in whom we can find shelter, protection and strength—not a place to hide in for ever, but a base from which to venture out with confidence, and to which we can return for safety and reassurance whenever we need. Sometimes it's hard to believe that the rock is still there to support us; but that rock has a way of turning up again when we reach rock bottom. ∎

Do take a moment to visit the *Quiet Spaces* website (www.quietspaces.org.uk) and email us with your thoughts, perhaps sparked by what you have read in this issue.

In our next issue

Next time, we turn to the theme of water. The cry of the psalmist was that he thirsted for God as 'in a dry and weary land where there is no water' (Psalm 63:1) and, in reflecting on some of the many ideas and images evoked by water, the eighth issue of *Quiet Spaces* will aim to offer refreshment for the parched soul.

Contact us at:

Quiet Spaces,
BRF, First Floor,
Elsfield Hall,
15–17 Elsfield Way,
Oxford OX2 8FG
enquiries@brf.org.uk

QUIET SPACES SUBSCRIPTIONS

Quiet Spaces is published three times a year, in March, July and November. To take out a subscription, please complete this form, indicating the month in which you would like your subscription to begin.

☐ I would like to give a gift subscription (please complete both name and address sections below)

☐ I would like to take out a subscription myself (complete name and address details only once)

This completed coupon should be sent with appropriate payment to BRF. Alternatively, please write to us quoting your name, address, the subscription you would like for either yourself or a friend (with their name and address), the start date and credit card number, expiry date and signature if paying by credit card.

Gift subscription name _____

Gift subscription address _____

_____

_____ Postcode _____

Please send beginning with the next July / November / March issue: *(delete as applicable)*

(please tick box)	UK	SURFACE	AIR MAIL
Quiet Spaces	☐ £16.95	☐ £18.45	☐ £20.85

Please complete the payment details below and send your coupon, with appropriate payment to: BRF, First Floor, Elsfield Hall, 15–17 Elsfield Way, Oxford OX2 8FG.

Name _____

Address _____

_____

Postcode _____ Telephone Number _____

Email _____

☐ Please do not email me any information about BRF publications

Method of payment: ☐ Cheque ☐ Mastercard ☐ Visa ☐ Maestro ☐ Postal Order

Card no. ☐☐☐☐ ☐☐☐☐ ☐☐☐☐ ☐☐☐☐ ☐☐☐☐ ☐☐

Valid from ☐☐☐☐ Expires ☐☐☐☐ Issue no. of Maestro card ☐☐☐

Security Code ☐☐☐

Signature _____ Date ___ / ___ / ___

All orders must be accompanied by the appropriate payment.
Please make cheques payable to BRF

PROMO REF: QSROCK

☐ Please do not send me further information about BRF publications

BRF is a Registered Charity